MW00580697

Printed in the United States of America

Published by ACB - Adult Coloring Books

ISBN 978-1-988245-08-9

Geometric Patterns

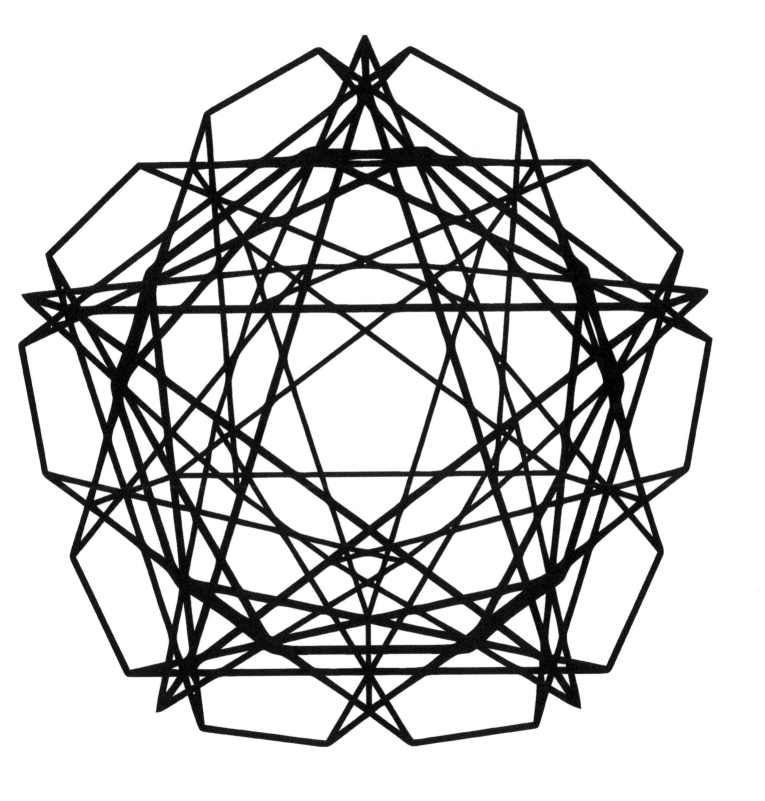

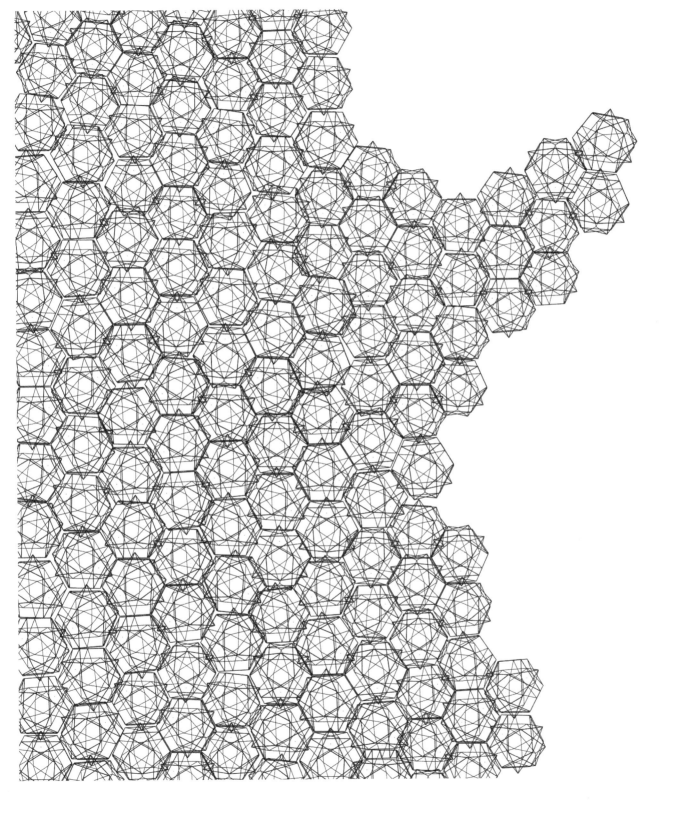

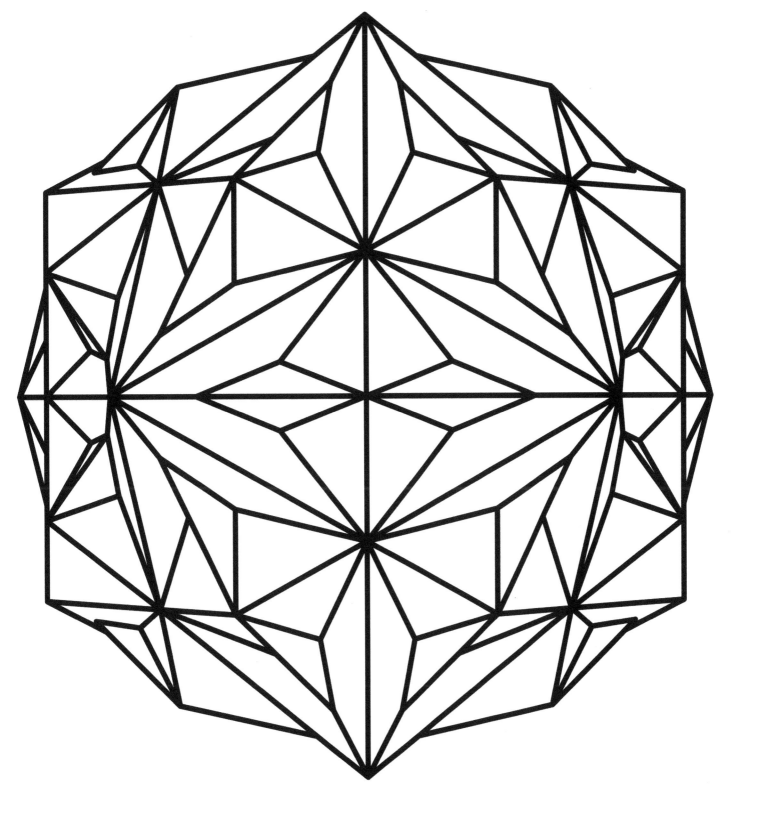

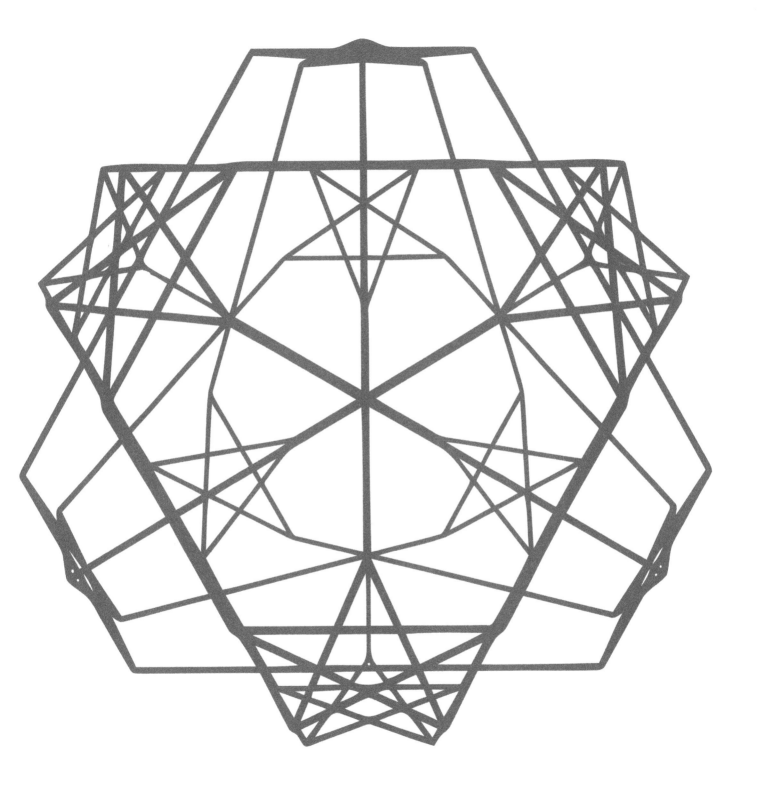

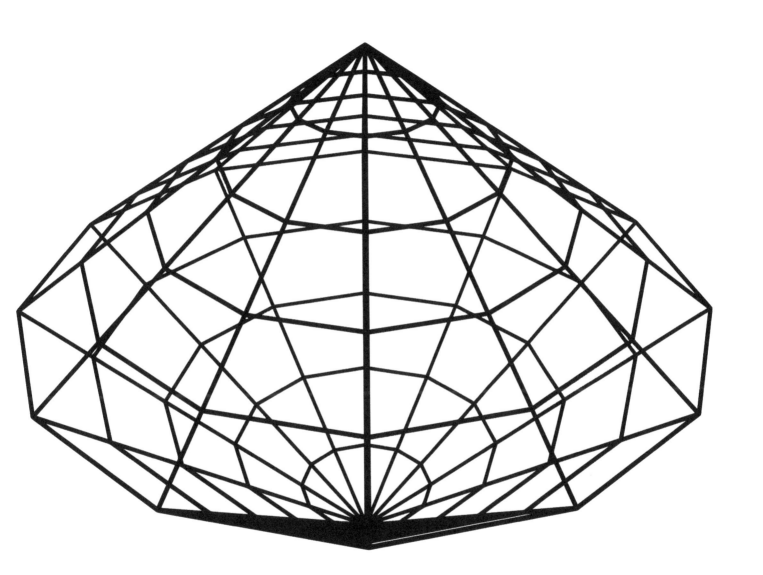

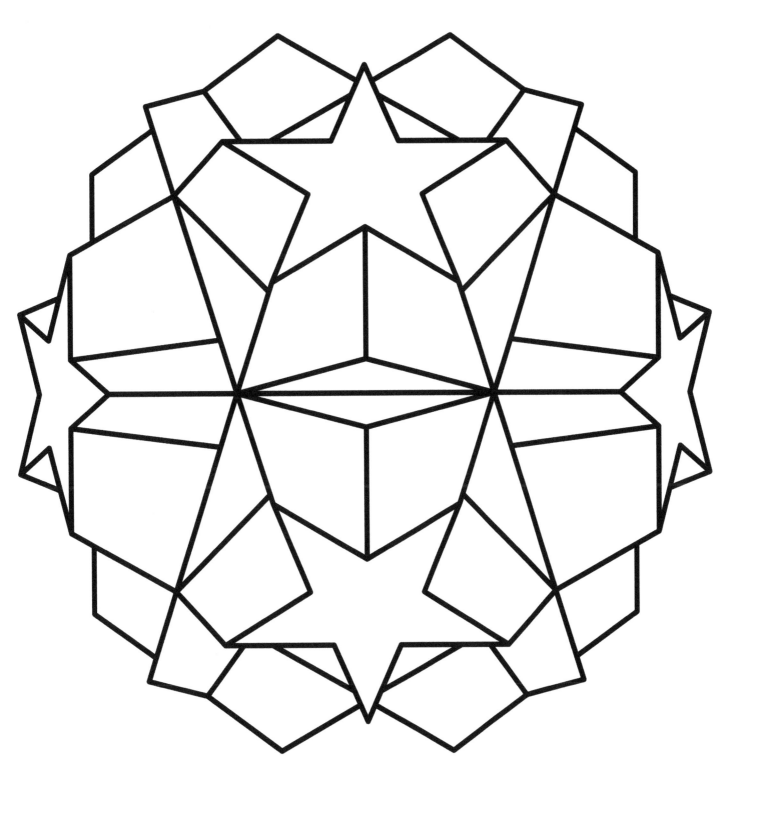

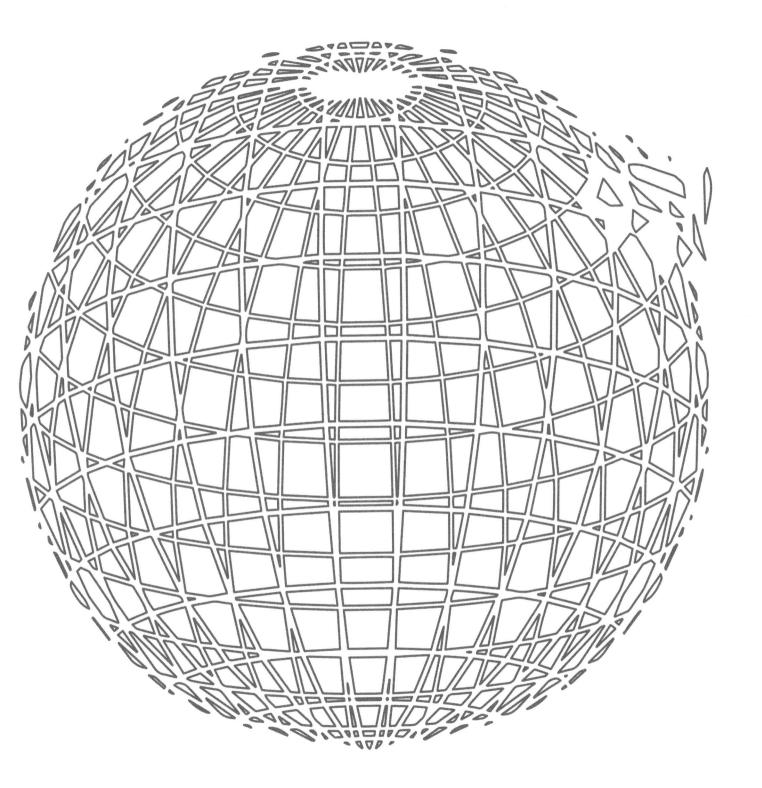

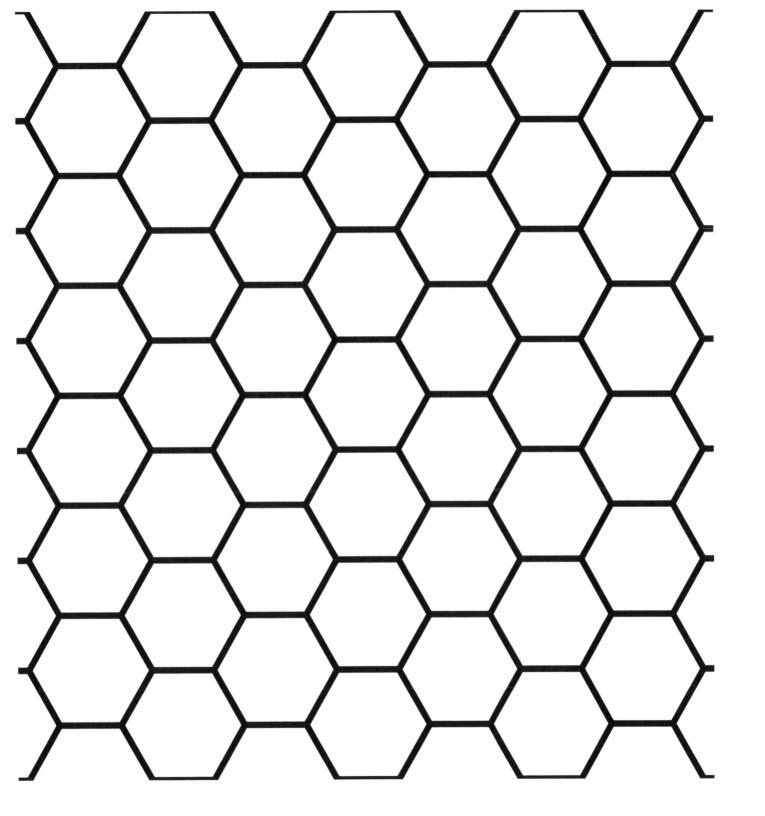

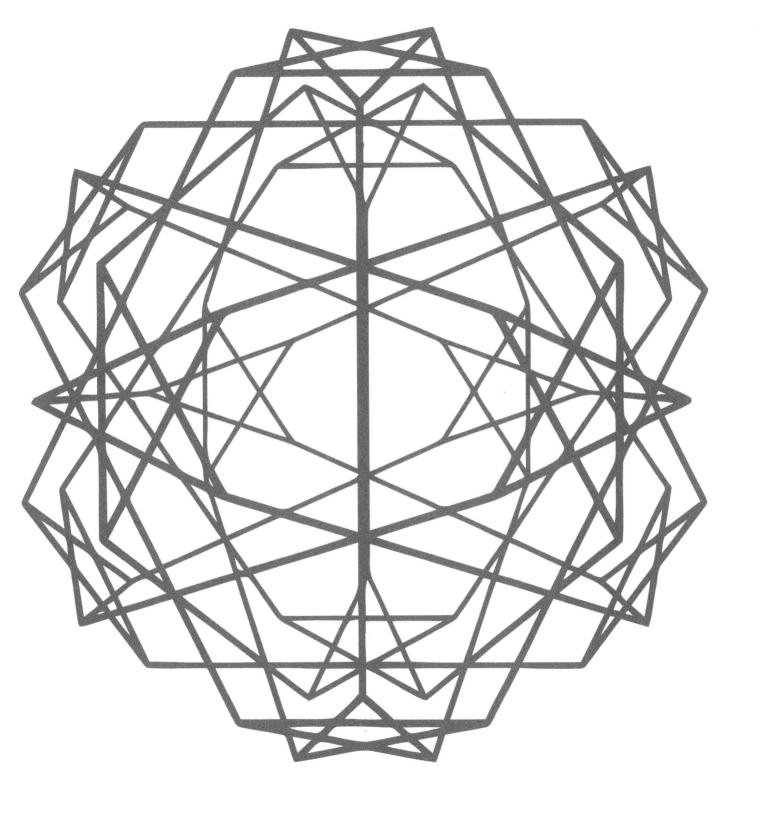

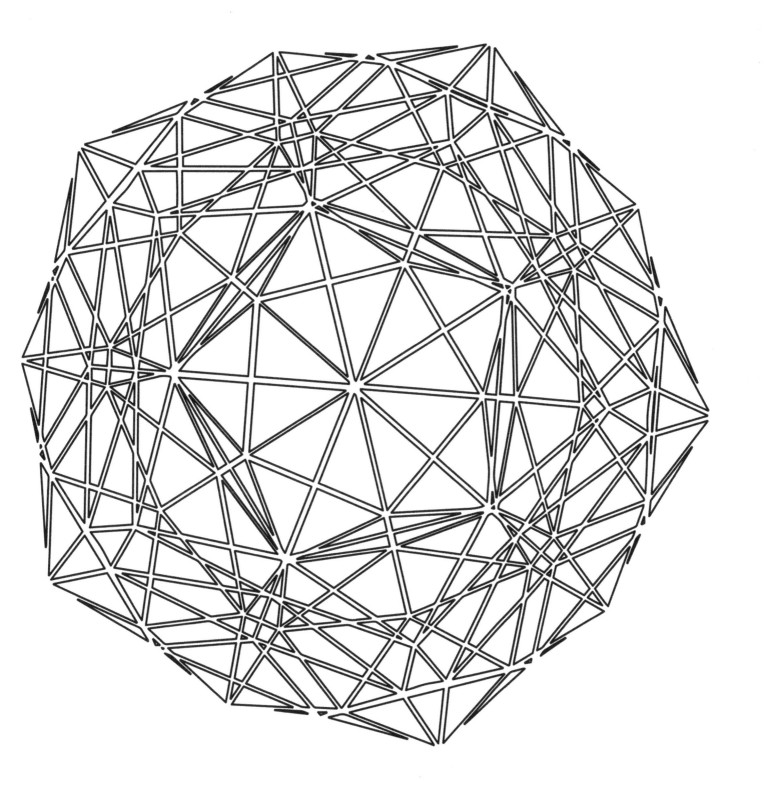

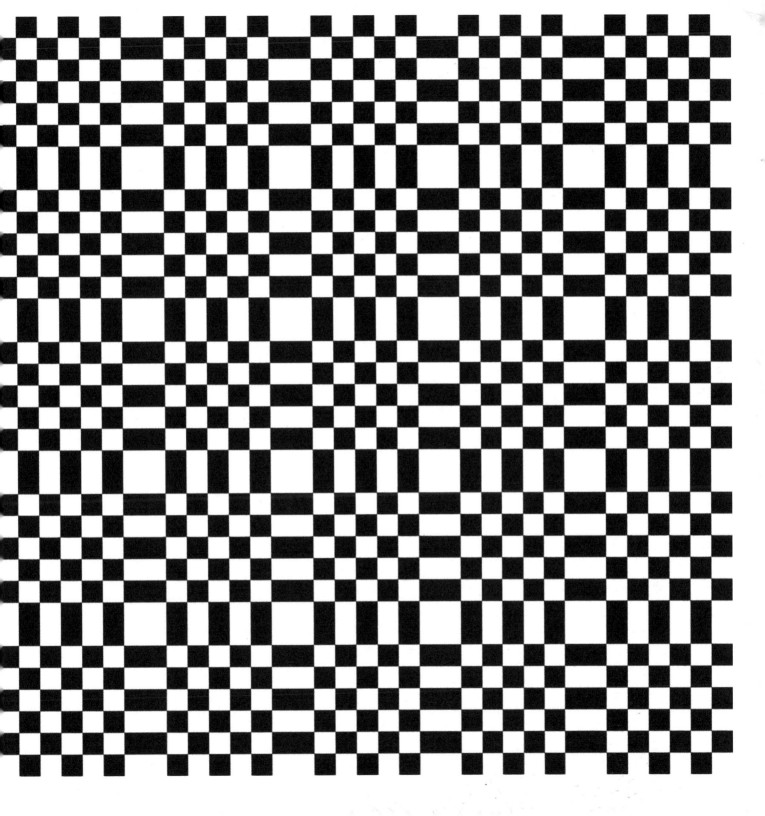

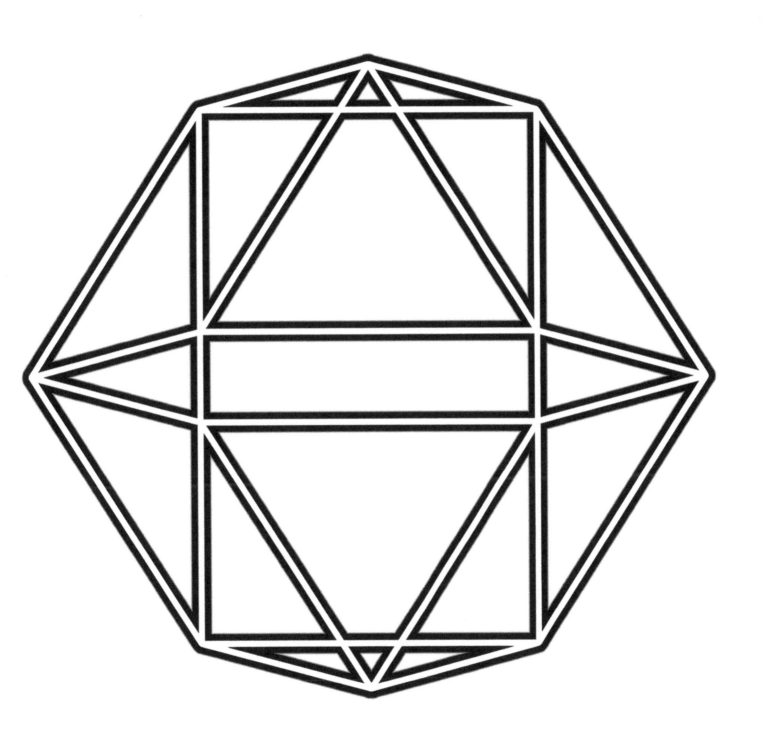

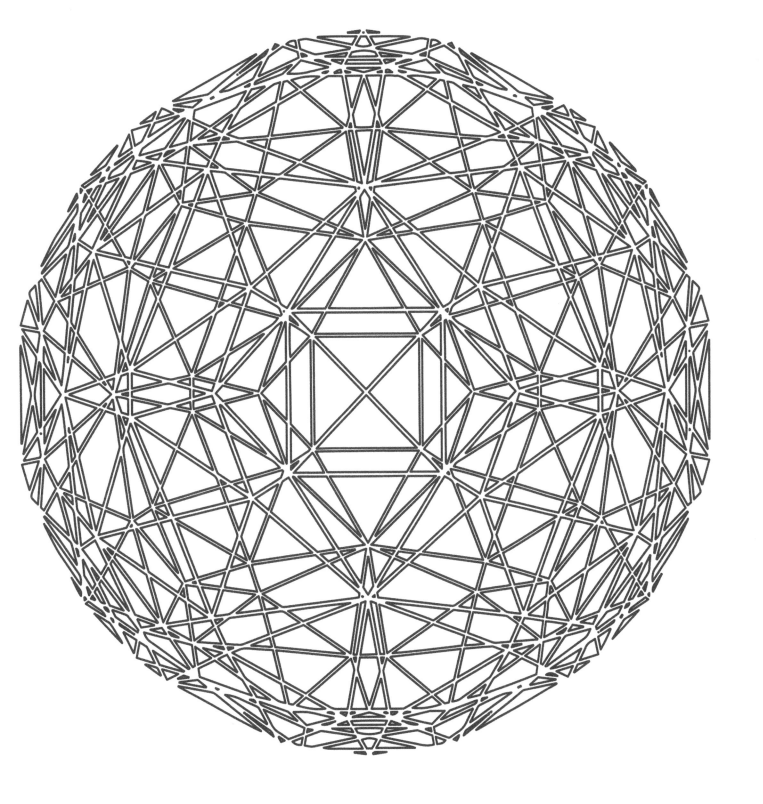

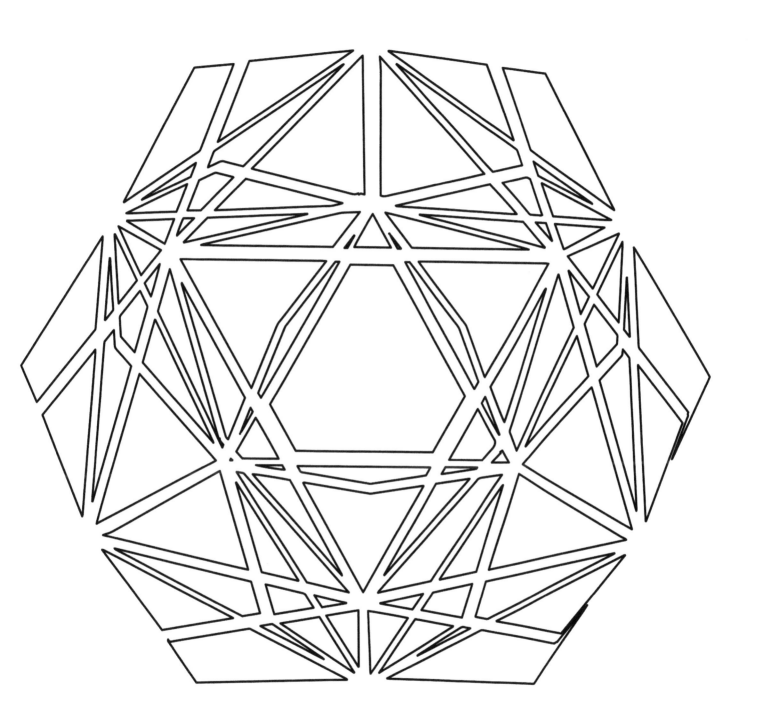

Mandalas

Celtic Designs

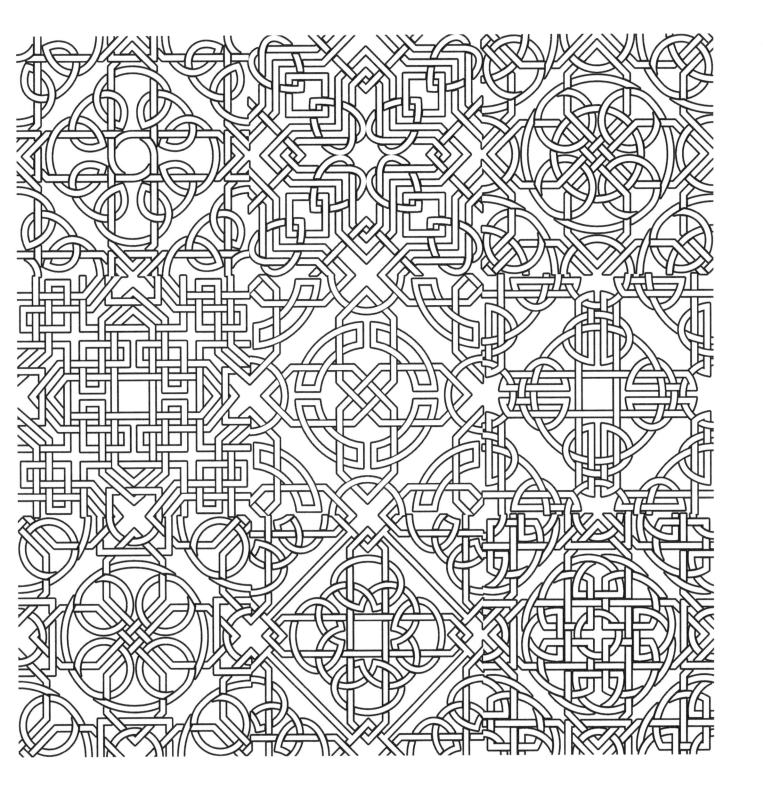

COLORING BOOKS BY ACB

CPSIA information can be obtained
at www.ICGtesting.com
Printed in the USA
LVHW060154170522
718975LV00013B/472